History's Yearbook

GIRL ACTIVISTS

Virginia Loh-Hagan

...ut I was free, and they should be free.
-Harriet Tubman

I am not afraid... I was born to do this.
-Joan of Arc

I am a queen. And as long as I live, I will reign.
-Zenobia

To create ... world in any ... arts takes c... ...age.
-Georgia O'Keeffe

A woman is like a tea bag. You can't tell how strong she is until you put her in hot water.
-Eleanor Roosevelt

The world has used me so unkindly. I fear it has made me suspicious of everyone.
-Mary Anning

Liberty!
–Inayat Khan's last word

If you hold your hand closed, nothing good can come in. The open hand is blessed, for it gives in abundance, even as it receives.
-Biddy Mason

... side of the room. I guess they didn't want to associate with me. But I could hold my own with them and sometimes did better.
-Mary Golda Ross

I've never been afraid in my life.
-Nancy Wake

I attribute my success to this: I never gave or took any excuse.
–Florence Nightingale

Women should be someone, and not something.
–Mary Cassatt

Well-behaved women seldom make history.
-Laurel Thatcher Ulrich

...ere is the day. We must welcome it with song.
–Marie Laveau

The title of Queen rang sweet to my ears.
-Catherine the Great

It's the little ...ings ... citizens do. T... will make th... My li... pl...
-V...

I0891862

Contents

Introduction

We are celebrating girl **activists**! Activists are fighters. They fight for human rights. They fight against things that are unfair. They fight for people who can't fight for themselves. They stand up against evil. They want things to change.

But their work is not easy. Many people try to stop them. Girl activists could get hurt. They put their lives at risk. They overcome many challenges. Challenges are hard tasks.

Throughout history, women have shown that they're tough. They're smart. They're strong. The girl activists in this book rise to the top. They paved the way for today's girl activists. You can be an activist, too. Stand up for what's right. Lead with your heart and mind. Be confident in your abilities. And refuse to give up.

Here's to you and all the girl activists in our lives!

chapter 1

BEST ALL-AROUND

Harriet Tubman

> But I was free, and they should be free.
>
> – Harriet Tubman

The "Best All-Around" award goes to Harriet Tubman. Tubman escaped **slavery**. Slavery is when people own other people. This is an unfair system. Tubman fought against slavery. She helped hundreds of slaves. She led them to freedom. She didn't lose a single person.

She did many other things. She fought in the U.S. Civil War. She led troops in battle. She was a cook. She was a spy. She was a nurse. She cured sicknesses. She knew the land. She knew plants. She knew how to make medicine. She helped sick soldiers.

She supported women's rights for equality. She opened up her house to the needy. She died in 1913.

chapter 2

MOST LOYAL

Dede Mirabal

> They all had an inner fire, a desire to get back up after getting pushed down. They managed to look deep inside themselves and find what they really and truly wanted.
>
> –Dede Mirabal

The "Most Loyal" award goes to Dede Mirabal. Mirabal was from the Dominican Republic. She and her 3 sisters were known as The Butterflies. They fought to overthrow Rafael Trujillo. Trujillo was a violent leader. Overthrow means to push out of power. Her 3 sisters were killed in 1960. They were beaten to death.

Unlike her sisters, Mirabal didn't go to college. She was a housewife. She ran the family business. She loved her sisters. She took care of their 6 children. She founded the Mirabal Sisters Museum. She wrote a book about their work. She traveled the world. She told their story. She wouldn't let people forget them.

chapter 3

MOST DISTINGUISHABLE VOICE

Coretta Scott King

> I am an activist. I didn't just emerge after Martin died. I was always there and involved.
>
> –Coretta Scott King

The "Most **Distinguishable** Voice" award goes to Coretta Scott King. Distinguishable means noteworthy. King was the wife of Dr. Martin Luther King Jr. Like her husband, she fought for civil rights. Civil means citizen.

She was also a singer. She studied music. She sang at church. She sang at concerts. Concerts are shows. She created Freedom Concerts. She performed at many places. She told stories about civil rights. She sang freedom songs. She used music to get people on her side. She gained support. She raised money.

She was musical in other ways. She played many instruments. She played piano. She played the trumpet. She played the violin.

chapter 4

MOST DETERMINED

Grace Lee Boggs

> We are struggling to change this country because we love it.
>
> –Grace Lee Boggs

The "Most **Determined**" award goes to Grace Lee Boggs. Determined means not quitting. Boggs was Chinese American. She died in 2015. She was 100 years old. She's the oldest activist. She kept fighting until her last day. She fought for civil rights. She fought for women's rights. She fought for better working and living conditions. She fought for the environment. She created community groups. She organized people. She spoke at events. She wrote books.

She lived in Detroit, Michigan. Her husband and friends were African American. She was devoted to building her city. She created Detroit Summer. This is a youth program. The youths fixed homes. They planted gardens. They hosted music festivals.

chapter 5

BIGGEST DREAMER

Victoria Woodhall

> I ask the rights to pursue happiness by having a voice in that government to which I am accountable.
>
> –Victoria Woodhull

The "Biggest Dreamer" award goes to Victoria Woodhull. Woodhull ran for U.S. president. She was nominated by the Equal Rights Party. She ran in 1872. She was the first woman to run for U.S president.

She was poor. She told people's fortunes for money. She sold healing mixes.

She and her sister opened a **stock** business. Stocks are ownership shares of a company. Woodhull was the first woman to buy and sell stock. She used her money to start a newspaper. She wrote articles supporting women's rights. Her writing shocked people. She was sent to jail for her writing.

chapter 6

EARTH'S BEST FRIEN

Wangari Maathai

It's the little things citizens do. That's what will make the difference. My little thing is planting trees. –Wangari Maathai

The "Earth's Best Friend" award goes to Wangari Maathai. Maathai won the Nobel Peace Prize in 2004. She was the first African woman to do so. In 2009, she was named a United Nations Messenger of Peace.

Maathai fought for the environment. She founded the Green Belt Movement. She protected nature. She worked with women to plant trees. She helped plant over 20 million trees. These trees were planted on farms, schools, and churches.

Maathai was from Kenya. Kenya is a country in Africa. She earned a doctorate. Doctorates are the highest degrees. Maathai was the first woman in East and Central Africa to do so.

chapter 7

MOST CARING

Lizzy Lind

> [I have] no objection to vivisection, provided that the vivisectors experiment on themselves.
>
> –Lizzy Lind

The "Most Caring" award goes to Lizzy Lind. Lind lived from 1878 to 1963. She was from Sweden. She fought for animal rights.

Scientists experiment on animals. They cut them open. Some did **vivisections**. This is cutting open living animals. Lind went to the London School of Medicine. She saw a brown dog being vivisected. This was called the "Brown Dog **affair**." Affair means event. Lind saw the dog in pain. She wrote about it. She got people to act. She founded a group to fight vivisection. She started a home for animals. She set up hospitals for horses hit in battle. She cared for animals her whole life.

chapter 8

MOST PROUD

Barbara Gittings

I discovered the power of the press. The power to put in what you want in order to influence readers. –Barbara Gittings

The "Most Proud" award goes to Barbara Gittings. Gittings spent a lot of time in libraries. She read many books. Some books described gay love as an illness. Gay means same sex. Gittings disagreed. She fought for gay rights. She was involved with the American Library Association. She wanted positive books about gay love. A book award was named for her.

Gittings fought against the medical community. She had them stop labeling gay love as an illness. This happened in 1972.

She organized a gay rights group in New York. There were bans against hiring gay people. Gittings fought against this. She marched. She held signs. She stood up for what she believed.

chapter 9

BEST TEAM

Susan B. Anthony and Elizabeth Cady Stanton

I forged the thunderbolts. [Anthony] fired them.

–Elizabeth Cady Stanton

The "Best Team" award goes to Susan B. Anthony and Elizabeth Cady Stanton. Anthony and Stanton were American **suffragists**. Suffragist are people who fight for the right to vote.

Anthony and Stanton met in 1851. They founded women's rights groups. They founded a newspaper. They traveled to many places. They fought for women's right to vote. They also fought against slavery.

They were a great team. Anthony was organized. She took care of business things. She came up with action plans. Stanton did most of the writing. She came up with ideas.

Anthony and Stanton helped each other. Stanton had seven children. Anthony was single. She helped take care of the children.

chapter 10

BEST YEARBOOK EDITOR

Amelia Jenks Bloomer

> Letters came pouring in upon me by hundreds from women all over the country making inquiries about the dress and asking for patterns—showing how ready and anxious women were to throw off the burden of long, heavy skirts. **–Amelia Jenks Bloomer**

The Best "Yearbook Editor" award goes to Amelia Jenks Bloomer. Bloomer was a suffragist. In 1848, she went to the Seneca Falls **Convention**. Convention means big meeting. This was the first women's rights convention. Bloomer worked on *The Lily*. This was the first newspaper by and for women. Bloomer took it over. She was the first woman to own, manage, and edit a newspaper for women.

She met a woman who wore pants. The pants were loose. They bunched up at the ankles. Bloomer liked them. She wore them. She promoted them in *The Lily*. She encouraged women to change how they dressed. She wanted women to dress more comfortably. The pants were called bloomers.

chapter

11

BEST SENSE OF HUMOR

Wilma Mankiller

> I never felt home until I came home. When I came back here, then I began to understand. This is where I belong.
>
> –Wilma Mankiller

The "Best Sense of Humor" award goes to Wilma Mankiller. Mankiller lived from 1945 to 2010. She fought for Native Americans and women. She was the first woman chief of the Cherokees. She helped her people. She improved health care. She improved education.

She joked about her name. She said, "Some people do earn their names in native culture. I didn't. But I don't always tell people that. Sometimes I just say that Mankiller is my name. I earned it. And I let them wonder." She was the only one who could joke about her name. She didn't like it when others did it.

Mankiller was a term of respect. It referred to an Indian fighter who guarded villages.

chapter 12

MOST LIKELY TO LEAD A PROTEST

Mother Jones

> You must stand for free speech in the streets. That is your right. And you must have it. –Mother Jones

The "Most Likely to Lead a Protest" award goes to Mary G. Harris Jones. Protests are events where people show disapproval of something. Jones is known as Mother Jones. She was a teacher. She also made dresses. She fought to improve working conditions. She organized people. She led **strikes**. Strikes were when people refused to work. People would go back to work if things got better.

Jones fought against child labor. Labor is work. She led a march. She walked 125 miles (201 kilometers). She marched from Philadelphia to President Theodore Roosevelt's home in New York. She wanted to show people how bad things were for child workers. She thought children should be in schools, not working. This happened in 1903.

Top Memories

- **1792:** British writer Mary Wollstonecraft published *A Vindication of the Rights of Woman*. Vindication means proof. Wollstonecraft said women should be treated fairly. She fought for women to be educated. This book was one of the earliest publications of feminism.

- **September 19, 1893:** New Zealand was the first country to grant women the right to vote. Australia did so in 1902.

- **September 1955:** Daughters of Bilitis (DOB) was formed. Bilitis was a female character. DOB was one of the first groups to fight for the rights of gay women. It was formed in San Francisco. It started as a small secret club. It grew to fight for civil rights.

- **January 16, 2006:** Ellen Johnson Sirleaf became president of Liberia. Liberia is a country in Africa. Sirleaf was the first female elected head of state in Africa.

Advice from the Field

Maya Angelou lived from 1928 to 2014. She was an African American poet. She was a civil rights activist. She worked with many black leaders. She worked with Dr. Martin Luther King Jr. She worked with Malcolm X. She worked with Nelson Mandela. She wrote many important books. She wrote about her life. She had a tough life. She grew up in a time that treated her unfairly. She was abused. She used her pain to help others. She fought for women. She fought for African Americans. She fought for gay rights. She was awarded the Presidential Medal of Freedom. She had many words of wisdom. She said, "If you don't like something, change it. If you can't change it, change your attitude." She also said, "People will forget what you said. People will forget what you did. But people will never forget how you made them feel."

Student Life & Clubs

Are you interested in being an activist? Consider the Harry Potter Alliance (HPA). Alliances are loyal teams. Andrew Slack founded the HPA. He's a Harry Potter fan. He turned fans into heroes. The HPA is a "creative and collaborative culture that solves the world's problems." It brings fans together. Fans fight for equality, human rights, and literacy. They've done many good things. They raised money to send supplies to people in need. They gave away many books. They launched a program called "What Would Dumbledore Do." They asked fans to tweet lessons learned from Harry Potter's teacher. J. K. Rowling is the author of the Harry Potter books. She said, "It's incredible. It's humbling. And it's uplifting to see people going out there and doing that in the name of your character."

"Well-behaved women seldom make history."

–Laurel Thatcher Ulrich

Did You Know...

- Malala Yousafzai became an activist in 2009. She was 12 years old. She fought for the education of girls. She's the youngest person to win a Nobel Peace Prize. She won it at age 17. She has an asteroid named after her. Asteroids are rocks that float around the sun.
- The feminist movement has had 3 waves. Waves are like stages. The first wave was focused on women's right to vote. The second wave focused on equal pay and women's bodies. The third wave focuses on diverse groups.

Learn More!

Calvert, Jennifer, and Vesna Asanovic (illust.). *Teen Trailblazers: 30 Fearless Girls Who Changed the World Before They Were 20*. New York: Castle Point Books, 2018.

Halligan, Katherine, and Sarah Walsh (illust.). *Herstory: 50 Women and Girls Who Shook Up the World*. New York: Simon & Schuster Books for Young Readers, 2018.

Staley, Erin. *The Most Influential Female Activists*. New York: Rosen Publishing, 2019.

Your Turn!

Now, it's your turn!
You get to choose the
"Top of the Class: Girl
Activist" winner.
Who would you pick?

TOP OF THE CLASS:
GIRL ACTIVIST

"Top of the Class" means being the best of the best. These prompts will help you think about who'd you pick for the "Top of the Class: Girl Activist" award:

- Why is this person the best "girl activist"? List reasons why this person deserves the award more than others.
- Think about how this person is different from girl activists in this book. What is special about this person?
- How is this person similar to girl activists in this book? Describe the qualities that girl activists should have. How does this person represent those qualities?
- How does this person make the world a better place? How does this person change history? Why should we remember this person?
- Girl activists often struggle. They may also face barriers. They're often told they can't do something. They don't run away when things get hard. How does your person overcome challenges?
- Activists fight against things that are unfair. What is unfair to your person? What are your person's causes? Causes are problems or issues. They need to be solved.
- Activists work in teams. They're stronger together. How does your person work with others?

Consider This!

TAKE A POSITION! Men and women should have equal rights. Do you think this is the case in today's world? Argue your point with reasons and evidence.

SAY WHAT? Explain what the activists have in common. What are they are fighting for? Explain how they're alike. Explain how they're different.

THINK ABOUT IT! What are some issues that you're passionate about? How can you make changes? Think of the activists presented in this book. What did you learn from them?

Glossary

activists (AK-tiv-ists) people who fight against things that are unfair in order to bring about change

affair (uh-FAIR) event

convention (kuhn-VEN-shuhn) big conference or meeting

determined (dih-TUR-mihnd) not willing to quit

distinguishable (dih-STING-gwishd) noteworthy

slavery (SLAY-vur-ee) unfair system in which one group of people own another group of people as property

stock (STAHK) ownership shares of a company

strikes (STRIKES) protests in which workers refuse to work until their conditions improve

suffragists (SUHF-rij-ists) people who fight for the right to vote

vivisections (vih-vih-SEK-shuhnz) the operations on or cutting open of live animals while they're awake

Index

45th Parallel Press

Published in the United States of America by Cherry Lake Publishing
Ann Arbor, Michigan
www.cherrylakepublishing.com

Reading Adviser: Marla Conn, MS, Ed., Literacy specialist, Read-Ability, Inc.
Book Designer: Jen Wahi

Photo Credits: ©Gotfryd, Bernard, photographer/Library of Congress/Reproduction No., LC-DIG-ppmsca-12437, cover (left), 8; ©Lindsley, Harvey B., photographer/Library of Congress/Reproduction No., LC-DIG-ppmsca-54232, cover (middle), 4; ©GL Archive/Alamy Stock Photo, cover (right), 12; ©Franciscocolombo/Wikimedia/Creative Commons Attribution-Share Alike 4.0 International, 6; ©Kyle McDonald/flickr, 10; ©Joseph Sohm/Shutterstock, 14; ©Archive PL/Alamy Stock Photo, 16; ©KAY TOBIN LAHUSEN/KRT/Newscom, 18; ©Edmonston, Washington, D.C., photographer/Library of Congress/Digital Id, http://hdl.loc.gov/loc.mss/mnwp.159001, 20; ©Science History Images/ Alamy Stock Photo, 22; ©Associated Press, 24; ©Bain News Service, publisher/Library of Congress, 26; various art pieces throughout courtesy of Shutterstock

45th Parallel Press is an imprint of Cherry Lake Publishing.

Library of Congress Cataloging-in-Publication Data

Names: Loh-Hagan, Virginia, author.
Title: Girl activists / by Virginia Loh-Hagan.
Description: [Ann Arbor : Cherry Lake Publishing, 2019] | Series: History's yearbook | Audience: Grades: 4 to 6. | Includes bibliographical references and index.
Identifiers: LCCN 2019004137| ISBN 9781534147911 (hardcover) | ISBN 9781534150775 (pbk.) | ISBN 9781534149342 (PDF) | ISBN 9781534152205 (hosted ebook)
Subjects: LCSH: Women political activists--Biography--Juvenile literature. | Women social reformers--Biography--Juvenile literature. | Women heroes--Biography--Juvenile literature.
Classification: LCC HQ1236 .L645 2019 | DDC 320.082--dc23
LC record available at https://lccn.loc.gov/2019004137

Printed in the United States of America
Corporate Graphics

About the Author:

Dr. Virginia Loh-Hagan is an author, university professor, former classroom teacher, and curriculum designer. She's an activist. She started a support group for Asian American female faculty and staff at San Diego State University. She lives in San Diego with her very tall husband and very naughty dogs.